First Facts™

Everyday Character Education

Honesty

by Kristin Thoennes Keller

Consultant:
Madonna Murphy, PhD, Professor of Education
University of St. Francis, Joliet, Illinois
Author, *Character Education in America's Blue Ribbon Schools*

Capstone
press

Mankato, Minnesota

First Facts is published by Capstone Press,
151 Good Counsel Drive, P.O. Box 669, Mankato, Minnesota 56002.
www.capstonepub.com

Library of Congress Cataloging-in-Publication Data
Thoennes Keller, Kristin.
    Honesty / by Kristin Thoennes Keller.
    p. cm.—(First facts. Everyday character education)
    Includes bibliographical references and index.
    ISBN-13: 978-0-7368-3681-4 (hardcover)
    ISBN-10: 0-7368-3681-0 (hardcover)
    ISBN-13: 978-0-7368-5149-7 (paperback)
    ISBN-10: 0-7368-5149-6 (paperback)
    1. Honesty—Juvenile literature. I. Title. II. Series: First facts. Everyday character education.
BJ1533.H7T48 2005
179'.9—dc22   2004020359

Summary: Introduces honesty through examples of everyday situations where this character trait
    can be used.

Editorial Credits
Amanda Doering, editor; Molly Nei, set designer; Kia Adams, book designer; Kelly Garvin,
    photo researcher

Photo Credits
Capstone Press/Karon Dubke, 15, 20
Dan Delaney Photography, cover, 1, 5, 6–7, 8, 9, 11, 12, 13, 19
Library of Congress, 16

Table of Contents

Honesty

Abby is one point behind in tennis. The **referee** didn't see where the ball landed. She asks Abby if the ball was in bounds or out. If Abby lies, she still has a chance to win. But she wants to win honestly. Abby tells the truth. The ball was in bounds.

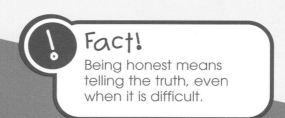

Fact!
Being honest means telling the truth, even when it is difficult.

At Your School

Honesty at school means doing your own work. Copying a friend's homework is **dishonest**. It is wrong to pretend you did the work yourself.

Be truthful at school. Don't accept **praise** for someone else's work. If you do not deserve a reward, say so.

Fact!
Classmates can learn to be honest from your example.

With Your Friends

Good friends are honest. If you break a friend's toy, tell her. Be honest and **apologize**. Follow the rules when playing games. Cheating is dishonest.

Honest people keep their **promises**.
If you promise to help a friend with his
homework, do it.

At Home

Family members are honest with each other. Tell the truth if you make a mess. You shouldn't blame it on your brother or sister.

Honest people do what they say. When you say you'll take out the garbage, do it right away.

Fact!

A friend may ask if you like her new haircut. You don't, but you can be honest without being mean. You can say that you liked her old haircut better. Being honest and nice is called using tact.

In Your Community

Be honest with people in your **community**. If a store clerk gives you too much change, give back the extra money.

Honest people return things they find. If you find a watch on the ground, take it to the police station. Someone is probably looking for it.

Herbert Tarvin

A truck carrying thousands of dollars tipped over in Miami, Florida. Money spilled out, and people grabbed it. Most people kept the money they found on the street. Eleven-year-old Herbert Tarvin was honest. He knew the money didn't belong to him. He returned the 85 cents he found to the police.

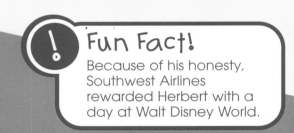

Fun Fact!
Because of his honesty, Southwest Airlines rewarded Herbert with a day at Walt Disney World.

Abraham Lincoln

Abraham Lincoln was the 16th U.S. president. He was known as "Honest Abe." As a young shop clerk, Lincoln found that he had charged a customer a few extra cents. At the end of the day, he walked several miles to the customer's house to return the money.

What Would You Do?

Abby forgot her math homework at home. Her teacher asked her why she didn't have the homework. Abby thought about making up a story. She could say her brother spilled juice on it. What is the honest thing for Abby to do?

Amazing but True!

In 1963, a Swedish teenager named Gulli Wihlborg lost her wallet. More than 40 years later, someone found her wallet and mailed it back to her. All her money, papers, and photos were still in the wallet.

Hands On: Lost-and-Found Box

Honest people return lost items when they find them. Make a lost-and-found box in your classroom. Your classmates can return the things they find.

What You Need

marker
large cardboard box

What You Do

1. With the marker, write "Lost and Found" on the box.
2. Put the box in your classroom where everyone can see it.
3. If you find something that isn't yours, put it in the box.
4. If you lose something, look in the box to see if someone has found it.

Glossary

apologize (uh-POL-uh-jize)—to say you are sorry

community (kuh-MYOO-nuh-tee)—a group of people who live in the same area

dishonest (diss-ON-ist)—not honest or fair

praise (PRAZE)—words telling someone they did a good job

promise (PROM-iss)—your word that you will do something

referee (ref-uh-REE)—a person at a sports event who makes sure players obey the rules

Read More

Bender, Marie. *Honesty Counts.* Character Counts. Edina, Minn.: Abdo, 2003.

Kyle, Kathryn. *Honesty.* Wonder Books. Chanhassen, Minn.: Child's World, 2003.

Internet Sites

FactHound offers a safe, fun way to find Internet sites related to this book. All of the sites on FactHound have been researched by our staff.

Here's how:
1. Visit *www.facthound.com*
2. Type in this special code **0736836810** for age-appropriate sites. Or enter a search word related to this book for a more general search.
3. Click on the **Fetch It** button.

FactHound will fetch the best sites for you!

Index